INIKI FRANKLIN

A GRACEFUL STORM

NAVIGATING THE STORMS OF LIFE
GRACEFULLY

Preface

Upon arriving at college in 2011, God told me that I would write a book, however, I did not know the details of when or how it would happen. Initially I doubted the idea of writing a book because in my mind I was not a writer. I could write, but to produce a book that would help many seemed far-fetched to me. Each year God confirmed, as He always does, the word that He spoke over my life. Weeks prior to writing the first chapters, God brought the idea back to my heart and mind at least twice a day. I stopped fighting Him on this project because I realized that writing this book really was not about me, but it was about God and all that He desired to do through it. In 2014, I began writing during a fast. The chapters rushed out of my fingertips like water. Never in my life had I thought this book would happen and yet, the manifestation of God's prophetic word in my life is here today.

Dear Reader,

My prayer is that God is well pleased with this book, and that your life is changed for the better. I hope that after reading this book you are able to weather the storms of life with poise and grace. I hope that Jesus shows you how to stay afloat and even to walk on water by empowering your soul to serve Him with all diligence. Ultimately, I anticipate a mighty move of God because of this book. Prayerfully it represents His name well to all people and that He receives all the glory, honor, and praise that is due to His holy name.

In Jesus' mighty name,

Amen.

Chapters

1. Ebb and Flow
2. Storm Tracking
3. Eye of the Storm
4. Through the Fog
5. Beacons of Sun
6. Hailstorms
7. Flash Floods
8. Aftermath
9. Clear Skies
10. A Graceful Storm

INTRODUCTION

Watching a storm roll in is a captivating phenomenon. Calmness permeates a gray sky and within moments, the wind begins to blow, temperatures shift, lightning illuminates the horizon, and thunder sounds the alarm of a storm that is well on its way. As frightening as storms are, you must admit that they are also breathtakingly beautiful. Life is also like this, full of storms that resemble the thunderstorms, heavy rains, hurricanes, tornadoes, monsoons, and typhoons we see in our lifetime. These storms progress through our lives with both beauty and destruction. Life as we understand it becomes altered, but heavy rains of trial and adversity provide clarity and purification.

Maybe you are in a great place and the clouds have not entered the horizon. Maybe you are in the midst of your storm, weathering it like a champ while taking on the downpours and pushing against the wind. Or, just maybe, the storms in your life are kicking your butt and you want to throw in the towel and call it quits. Like all scenarios in life, storms have a divine timestamp on them. You are not going to remain in the same situation forever!

What I learned at a very young age, and what I continue to learn, is that grace is a very important gift from God that helps you through every storm in your life. A lot of times we do not actively think about the deep importance of grace, we just know that we have it through Jesus. However, I challenge you to digest the grace God gives you. Grace is like the finest of linens or silks. Grace is gentle, yet strong. Grace allows you to go through trials with strength when you feel weak. Grace does internal work. Grace allows you to smile when your heart is hurting. Grace allows you to go further than ever imagined. Grace is the epitome of Christ's anointing in our lives. Grace helps us to do what we otherwise cannot do. Grace covers where we mess up and fall short. Most of all, grace shows us that God's love for us is abundant and endless, not conditional.

Whether you are entering a storm, weathering a storm, or leaving a storm, the key to getting through gracefully is to remember the purpose behind it and the presence of God in it. The grace of God is your strength within a storm. 2 Corinthians 12:9 asserts that the Lord's strength is the perfect solution to our weakness. His strength is the perfect solution to our storms. It is a reassurance that we do not have to lean on our own strength within our challenges. We do not have to try to handle the cares of life by ourselves! Be confident in Him and stand firm on the promises of His word, both written and spoken to you. If you do not yet know this amazing God that provides comfort in the midst of a storm, then you should get to know Him. He is full of amazement and wonder.

1

Ebb and Flow

The imperfection of humanity constantly reminds us that we are in need of a perfect savior. Whether we realize it or whether we choose to ignore the call on our hearts, God has so much more to offer us than the bare minimum that we often ask of Him. There comes a point in life when human effort fails and things become dry, stale, and unsatisfying. You are living your life, business as usual, then BAM, things are not the same with the Lord as they once were. You begin to notice that your appetite has changed. That spark of joy you had while serving is now gone. You've wandered away from your first love just like the waves in the ocean recede from the shore. This is what I describe as the 'ebb' of your storm.

Ezekiel 37: 1-14 portrays it best. In this story the Lord leads Ezekiel to the top of a valley and this valley is full of dry bones. The Lord asks him a rather complex question, "Can these dry bones live?" Ezekiel says, "Lord you alone know whether the dry bones can live." The Lord asked him this question twice. This is an important distinction because to me, it indicates that Ezekiel's first response may have contained doubt, disbelief, or a little bit of shock. The Lord did not change his question to Ezekiel though, instead He asks again. Ezekiel answers again with the same response and the Lord then provides instruction. He is directed to speak to the dry bones and *command* them to live. Ezekiel obeys and speaks to the dry bones and they come to life. The Lord then goes on to tell him how He (The Lord) will restore the people of Israel. Besides the miracle Ezekiel witnessed, this was a huge deal because the people of Israel had lost hope. They were essentially dead. God made a promise to him of restoration and fulfillment, but he had to open his mouth and speak life to a dead situation. I imagine when the Lord asked him the same question again that he came to a deeper understanding of what the Lord was asking him: Do you have faith to *believe* that these dry bones can live again?

Part of enduring your storm gracefully is understanding that God can and will restore anything that you've lost according to His will for your life. Relationships, families, jobs, hopes, dreams, and vision-- God can breathe on all of it. What you are responsible for is opening your mouth and declaring, in faith, life over that which is lifeless. You are responsible for the sowing. Often, we know that God can do much for our circumstances, but we struggle believing that He will do it for us *individually*. Why is that? During pivotal moments when God asks you, *"Can these dry bones live again,"* what is your answer? Your answer within these moments will place you on a trajectory of change taking you from the ebb in your life and catapulting you into your flow.[1]

"For I know the plans I have for you," declares the Lord, "plans to prosper you and not to harm you, plans to give you hope and a future. Then you will call on me and come and pray to me, and I will listen to you. You will seek me and find me when you seek me with all your heart." Jeremiah 29:11-13

God has plans for us. Good plans. Great plans. Mind-blowing plans. In order to find the

---

[1] Scriptures: Ezekail 37: 1-14;Jeremiah 29:11-13; John 15:5; (Reference scriptures: Matthew 11:28; John 6:37; James 4:8)

satisfaction that comes with those plans, we have to seek Him with our whole heart. If we do not want God, we cannot know God. If we do not know God, we will never give Him permission to move in our lives. If we never give Him permission to move in our personal lives, nothing will change. We will remain in a constant ebb with no flow, always receding, but never fully embracing His love. God gives us a choice. He always places a desire in us for Him, but sometimes we resist this desire so that we can do what we want to do. Deeply wanting God comes from, not only a place of worship, but also a place of hunger. How hungry are you?

God never intended for us to dwell in a place of deprivation because He makes Himself extremely accessible. (James 4:8) Sometimes we choose to deprive our spirits until we have little energy left to fight. Our spiritual appetite begins to scratch at our ankles, and we see how far we've wandered from the Lord. This is not spoken in a condemning way, but definitely in the mode of conviction because many of us have been in a place of deprivation while lacking a hunger for God and His righteousness. We get our fill from God and then wander away again until we cannot take it any longer. God wants us out of this cycle of deprivation and wants us to dive into the waters of hunger and thirst for Him. I cannot promise a lot, but I can promise you this, the Lord will satiate you in a way that you have never experienced before.

Apart from God we can accomplish nothing (John 15:5). My college pastor once stated that God desires "reckless abandonment." That recklessness is what causes us to hungrily cry out to God from the depths of our soul. It is the forsaking of everything common, and the embracing of the uncommon, supernatural power of God. It is shifting in the ocean as the waves of His spirit crash over you. It may seem like you are drowning, but God keeps you afloat. Reckless abandonment says to God that you trust Him with everything. It says that you will forsake the comfort of the known for a moment with Him in the unknown. He understands well that the unknown is not desirable. He also understands that when our human intellect fails us, that we need to be brought back into full faith and trust in Him. He is not afraid of our humanity. This means that whether we feel the passion for God or not, we must still cry out to God from a deep, authentic place. We must still yearn for Him; We must long for Him as if we are in a desert. He is the only one that can satisfy the depths of our souls. Let your deep cry out to His deep. Allow Him to satiate and sustain you in new ways during your storm. Allow him to restore proper balance to your life and move you out of the ebb and into His flow.

Challenge: Ask yourself the following question: What does a life of fulfillment look like for me? Write down your answer.

Remember: If you come to Him, He will receive you. If you seek Him with your whole heart, you will surely run into Him. If you draw close to Him, He will draw close to you.

2

Storm Tracking

There is beauty in the destruction; it is a humbling process that brings us to our knees.

Storm trackers are trained professionals that know how to detect, monitor, and handle a storm. They chase and observe these beautiful disasters because they know that insight will be provided on how to better navigate the next one. Storm trackers know how to survive moments of danger. They know when to step down and allow them to pass through. Storm trackers operate on hope that change will manifest. Most importantly, storm chasers have a methodical plan for chasing their storms. It is not randomized, but strategic. Just like these trained professionals, when life hits hard, it is best to ask the Lord for wisdom and discernment on how to track your storm. It is imperative that you seek instruction on what to do and how to do it. Clarity comes when we confide in the Lord. He always has a plan. "Keep on asking, and you will receive what you ask for. Keep on seeking, and you will find. Keep on knocking, and the door will be opened to you." (Matthew 7:7 NLT)

I've always been an independent person--even as a child. I had to learn how to be an interdependent person and ask for help as an adult which did not happen until I came into Christ and gained a deeper understanding of how much I actually needed Him and others. As the middle child of my family, somewhere along the line I learned the lie that I had to figure out life for myself. I learned that needing help was somehow a burden or wrong. I learned how to be quiet and to suffer in silence even though there were people in my life that held a wealth of wisdom, knowledge, and understanding. Not to mention, they actually *wanted* to help. Now let me be clear, my childhood was not horrible. In fact, my childhood was pretty good. It was healthy and I always had my needs met. So, I often wonder, "When did I learn the lie that I have to be self-sufficient? When did I learn that it was only up to me to make things happen?" The Lord began to dismantle these lies by allowing me to go into some tough situations that I could not get myself out of. More was needed besides my limited view of self and thought process. I needed the grace of God, and I did not even realize it.

"And He said to me, 'My grace is sufficient for you, for My strength is made perfect in weakness.' Therefore most gladly I will rather boast in my infirmities, that the power of Christ may rest upon me." (2 Corinthians 12:19) While independence and self-motivation are necessary components of a matured life; we cannot live life alone. We are not meant to function in silos, so it is quite imperative that we rely on others to walk out our storms with us. Even more, it is critical that we allow the Holy Spirit to lead us. Its literal function is to be our helper. In John 14:15-21, Jesus is speaking with His disciples about the Holy Spirit and how He will be an advocate for them. Jesus tells them this before one of the most tumultuous storms in all humanity; His crucifixion. There was a reason why the Lord promised His Holy Spirit to His people. In the midst of all of the pain and suffering, He knew that His people would need an anchor in order to continue to do the work of the kingdom. Crucifixion was one of the most shameful and horrific ways to die, yet Jesus took what was shameful and conquered it. I can only imagine how precious the promise was to His disciples and close loved ones at the point of his death.

For them, this was a real live execution of someone that they loved and did life with. I can only imagine just how much their humanity was fighting with their spirits during this time. Yet, they had a promise on the other side of His death that the Holy Spirit would come and be with them. We need the Holy Spirit just as badly now as they needed Him back then. The beauty of His still small voice and the unction of His love moves the clouds of uncertainty away. The discernment and intuition we feel to move towards or away from ideas, opportunities, or self-driven dreams are byproducts of the Holy Spirit's help. He is indeed an advocate that will go to bat for us. He is indeed the helper that will provide revelation if we seek it out. He is the one that helps us track and make it through our challenges.

Take a Moment:

What specific questions do you have for the Holy Spirit regarding your life?

Now ask Him. He will freely give you the clarity you need. Be patient and wait for the Lord to come.

3
Eye of the Storm

*"And the **peace** of God, which **surpasses** all understanding, will guard your hearts and your minds in Christ Jesus." (Philippians 4:7 ESV)*

For most of us, the brashness of our storms draw out questions for the Lord. What will the outcome look like? Is there something more I can do? What should I do while I'm here? How can I get out of this? Our humanity tells us that we are in danger and that we have reason to panic. Our spirit tells us to wait on the Lord and to trust that things will turn out better than expected. This is a consistent war that we must tackle within our unique trials. Sometimes we react and other times we retract when in reality, we should stand confidently in the Lord's instruction and promise.

Typically, the most tranquil region of a storm is directly in the middle of it. This region is called the "eye" of a storm. Surrounded by chaos and destruction, it is the only place that does not reflect its surroundings. When we think about a severe storm, there should be no areas of relief.

It does not make sense logically. Peace and chaos are polar opposites, yet they need one another to exist. However, just like it says in Philippians 4:7, God's peace surpasses all understanding. Not just some understanding, but ALL understanding. What does not make sense to us, makes total sense to the Lord. The Lord wants us to grasp that He is the eye of whatever storm you endure in this lifetime. He is the area of peace that you can take refuge in when everything around you is falling apart. Peace in the middle of a storm reflects the Lord's sustaining power. It can have many forms. Sometimes it looks like stillness and rest and other times it looks like action, decision, and operation in the wisdom of the Lord.

2 Kings 4:1-7 shows us how the Lord sustained a widow and her son in the midst of an uncertain time. His provision resulted in divine peace and provision for this woman and her family, but she had to trust and be obedient to instructions that would seem irrational and crazy to the average person. She had to do something that surpassed all understanding. In this story, a widow approached Elisha the prophet for help. She explains to him that her husband, who was now deceased, was a man

that honored the Lord in his lifetime. She explains to Elisha how creditors were coming to take away her sons to make them slaves. This alone tells me that this woman was left in a significant amount of debt following the death of her husband. During biblical times, women did not have independence, so with her husband being dead and the threat of her two sons being taken away, this woman would have been left destitute with no male covering and/or viable resources. She petitions Elisha with these facts and Elisha asks the woman what it is in her house. Wait a minute, that's an odd question to ask a widow who was in a state of panic. Her husband is dead, creditors are threatening to take her sons, and when she seeks help, she is met with a question of what she has. Now, one can imagine how this woman must have looked at Elisha. I envision this woman with a look of uncertainty, maybe a mix of disbelief and desperation. Nevertheless, she answers his question and tells him that she only has oil. The inflection of her 'only' tells me that she was not able to see the resourcefulness of the oil she possessed. Elisha tells her to borrow vessels from her neighbors, as many as she can gather. He instructs her to shut the door behind her with her sons and begin to pour out her oil into vessels. Now this was this widow's last of everything. Nevertheless, she operated in obedience and did what Elisha said to do. As she poured into the vessels, she was able to fill up every single one. She ended up running out of vessels and at that point the oil stopped. She is then instructed to go and sell the oil, pay off the debt, and live off the rest. This is what I call a miracle.

This woman was experiencing a major storm filled with uncertainty and lack. Little did she know that she was anointed to handle the challenge. Little did she know just how much the Lord would provide. God met this woman with a wise plan of action through his prophet to ensure that the chaos around her ceased. No longer did she have to worry about her sons being taken away due to debt. No longer did she have to worry about lack; the Lord gave her an abundance. It was in her obedience that this happened. Just like this woman, in the middle of your storm the Lord will provide an abundance for you to pour out. Sometimes the Lord will require action from you. Just like this woman, the Lord may be asking you to move on an idea, dream, or gift that he has placed in you. The Lord may be asking you to simply allow him to be your peace in the middle of your storm. Remember and know that you are anointed to endure this life by God's grace. Sometimes while we are in our trials we cannot see what's been provided as a relief. I challenge you to look at your trial and see where your oil lies. What resources, both material and spiritual, do you have to get you through your challenges?

Exercise:

Write down your resources, both material and spiritual. Then ask the Lord how to use these resources within your life.

4
Through the Fog

Fog, in its basic composition, is nothing more than water droplets or ice that has sort of condensed into a low-hanging cloud. It dissipates in sunshine and lingers over bodies of water. As simplistic as water droplets and ice sound, fog can become thick enough to completely obstruct your view. The only way to navigate fog is to go directly through it. There are no shortcuts. Sometimes our walk with Christ is a lot like navigating through fog. We have all that we need to arrive at our destination, yet at times we can only see what is directly in front of us. We only have enough strength to turn on the headlights. We only have enough courage to drive 10 mph. Fog is exactly what we need to build Godly character because it evokes trust. When you cannot see, and when life does not make any sense, you have to believe and push through. "The unknown is God's territory." - Pastor Deandre Green

The Lord taught me about pushing through the fog while I was a graduate student. After spending four years at The University of West

Georgia, building lifelong friendships, and thriving in campus ministry, leaving my college town left me feeling like a fish out of water. I remember the day that I moved from Carrollton and back to Atlanta clearly. It was highly emotional for me and full of tears. It was emotional because one chapter of my life closed and although I knew the next chapter, I did not know what the next chapter held. I did not know what graduate school would be like. The adjustment to a new routine and creating a new normal was a challenge. Education came naturally to me, so I worried more about my social life and building healthy friendships because everyone needs friends; and as I learned, you especially need friends in graduate school. The mental, physical, and emotional stress of performing at a higher level was overwhelming at times. I can honestly say that graduate school was a time when I felt most alone. Although all my friends were still in Georgia, it simply was not the same. Community was not the same and I often struggled to see the end goal as to why I needed a degree in Social Work anyway. Not only did my community change, I moved into new student apartments where I knew no one. My roommates all went to different colleges and that was even more isolating. I like to think that I am a cool person but meeting new people and making new friends was downright intimidating. So, this time was foggy for me. This was a time where I struggled with my humanity more than ever. I can be transparent and say that my flesh was at an all-time high. Things that definitely did not reflect my life while in Carrollton were extremely present. I was a different person at the time. This was a time where the only thing I could do was rely on God in a new way to guide me through because life seemed so obscure. I did not feel like myself at all. I felt like I was wandering through just hoping that the next step was on solid ground. I was hard on myself for every little thing I did wrong and I tried so hard to fit in with people. Eventually, God gave me community while in graduate school. He gave me quality friends and awesome professors. I landed a job that I did not think I would ever do and that was property management. Surprisingly, I was good at it. I developed a new sense of identity and the inward storm that I had been experiencing began to subside. I left graduate school confident and ready to tackle the next chapter of my life. It just taught me that the fog does clear in time.

"The Lord directs the steps of the godly. He delights in every detail of their lives. Though they may stumble, they will never fall, for the Lord holds them by the hand." (Psalm 37:23-24 NLT) You are not alone as you travel through the foggy moments in your life. God knows where the pitfalls are, specifically the ones designed for your life. The Lord is well aware of our individual needs. He knows where the cracks in the ground lie, so why not trust Him and boldly walk into the unknown? We must trust His heart. Many times, we will accuse God of not providing instructions or not providing clarity when in reality He already has. He already stated clearly in His word that trusting in Him leads us to where we need to be. We have to accept the challenge and be brave. "Your word is a lamp to guide my feet and a light for my path." (Psalms 119:105 NLT) Just like the headlights on a car illuminate a path as you drive through fog, so does the Holy Spirit illuminate the path of our life. Little by little the full picture will come into focus. We may get a word one day that finally makes sense years later. God is intentional with providing us with what we can handle at a moment's notice. He provides what we are ready for. All that He is looking for in His people is trust and faithfulness in who He is. God's word is a love letter full of promises; God does not lie. It is that simple. In the unknown, we must choose to put our faith and trust in God. Why must we do this? Putting your faith and trust in God does the following:

1. Gives Him free reign in our lives
2. Removes *self* out of the way
3. Serves as an act of obedience to His word

If you try to navigate the unknown in your own strength, you will find yourself:

- Tired
- Stressed out
- Emotionally drained
- Emotionally unstable
- Angry
- Frustrated
- Skeptical/unsure/double minded

- In a state of sin/transgression/iniquity

God did not call us to try to figure out everything ourselves. He calls for us to cast our cares upon Him, to commit our plans to Him, and to wait patiently for Him to move according to His will, not ours. (1 Peter 5:7; Proverbs 16:3; Isaiah 40: 31; Psalms 27:14) I want to encourage you that if you are in a place where everything looks foggy that God really has everything under control. God knows that we are fragile humans. I also want you to take a moment to repent for not trusting the Lord at His word if you haven't been. It is okay, we have all gone through this at one point or another on various levels. God is the only one that will forever be faithful to His word. Search for Him in His word and get to know Him more. The beauty of the unknown is that it causes us to get to know God in a different way. He has placed you in that area for you to search out His heart, to become more intimate with Him, and to relinquish control to Him. He is working behind the scenes, and in due time He will reveal His plan for your life.

"Trust in the Lord with all of your heart and lean not on your own understanding. In all of your ways acknowledge him and He will direct your path." (Proverbs 3:5 NKJV)

Pray and profess these words from your heart:

God you are good! Everything good and perfect comes from you. (James 1:17) I do not have to worry, nor do I have to fret about what will come of my life. My life belongs to you, and to you only. You have already ordained my steps. You have already ordered the path of my life. It is a perfect path that leads to you. It may be bumpy, it may be rocky, I may have to cry, I may have to crawl, but I will not stop pursuing you. Though it may get foggy, I will not stop pursuing your heart. Lord, give me the trust, faith, and patience to wait on you and know that you are moving on my behalf. I live to seek you, I live to worship you, and I live to honor you. Lord, in this season, let me become more intimate with you. Allow me to sink deep into the waters of your spirit. Holy Spirit, guide me like only you know how to do. Minister to me in my low points. Breathe into me when I feel deflated. Breathe into me when I feel lifeless. Remind me of who you are when I am tempted with fear and worry. Break every stronghold that would keep me in a place of worry and fear. I put my trust in you, and in you alone. I do not put my trust in my money, my family, my friends, my job, or the government, I put my total trust in you, Lord. Lord, I thank you for who you are. I thank you for being the gracious and great God that you are. I thank you, Lord almighty, that I am yours.

In Jesus' name I have prayed,

Amen.

5

Beacons of Sun

"It came to pass in the month of Chislev, in the twentieth year, as I was in Shushan the citadel, that Hanani one of my brethren came with men from Judah; and I asked them concerning the Jews who had escaped, who had survived the captivity, and concerning Jerusalem. And they said to me, 'The survivors who are left from the captivity in the province are there in great distress and reproach. The wall of Jerusalem is also broken down, and its gates are burned with fire.' So it was, when I heard these words, that I sat down and wept, and mourned for many days; I was fasting and praying before the God of heaven." (Nehemiah 1: 1-4 NKJV)

I like to think of Nehemiah as a hope builder. He sees shambles and ruins, but still accepts the challenge to build. Nehemiah had a position of importance, stature, and authority, not one that he could easily abandon. He was the king's cupbearer which meant that he needed to be present in the palace at all times. His story opens with news of his people and hometown being in ruins. Historically,

Nehemiah's ancestors strayed from the Lord and adopted a pagan lifestyle which ultimately led to this end result of ruin. Many had gone before Nehemiah with hopes of restoring their land. The news of his hometown breaks Nehemiah's heart and he cries out to the Lord.

One day, as he is doing his job as cupbearer, the king notices that he is sad. This is not the countenance that he typically has so the king asks him what is wrong. Nehemiah is careful in response, but truthful. He tells the king that the town of his father, his origin, is in ruins. The king then asks Nehemiah, "What do you want to do about it then?" Nehemiah says that he wants to go back and rebuild what was destroyed. The king grants his requests, but not only does he grant his request, he provides special orders (documents, permits) to Nehemiah in anticipation of barriers that he would face. Nehemiah anticipates that people will try to stop him and prepares for the upcoming opposition. We see through his courage, the beginning stages of restoration.

Sometimes the Lord will ask you to build when it is difficult. Sometimes He will ask you to take on a task where it seems like you are the only one that cares about it. He will ask you to trust Him through the pain. He will ask you to try even when you cannot predict the outcome. He will ask you to build in the presence of direct opposition. Just like a doctor offers physical therapy for further mobility of joints and muscles, so does the Lord desire to build our strength through challenges. The resistance builds character and faith. "Faith is the substance of things hoped for and the evidence of things not yet seen." (Hebrews 11:1) Nehemiah believed that the walls would be rebuilt in the face of scrutiny, mocking, corruption and direct assault.

Have you ever felt like the only hope builder within your family or immediate circle of influence? Have you ever felt like the only one that sees the vision beyond reality and beyond what the outcome looks like it is supposed to be? Have you ever been the only one advocating that change is possible and that things can be different if only there were a strategy to navigate the brokenness? I believe Nehemiah felt all these emotions while trying to be obedient to the burden on his heart for restoration. There was a promise attached to his storm. Nehemiah knew that fixing what was broken would have a domino effect on future generations. He was not merely doing it for himself, but for those that would come after him as best as he could.

God will have you build in the middle of your storm so that your light shines for those that are in complete and utter darkness. The light that comes from your work towards the kingdom and your purpose will inspire others. The world is waiting to see how we handle challenges as believers. There is a unique dichotomy that we are able to present because of Christ. We are able to show hope in the midst of hopelessness, joy in the midst of sorrow, healing in the midst of pain, and creativity in the midst of stagnancy.

There is much required of us, but nothing that cannot be accomplished. The labor that you exude during your storm is not in vain. The fruit that will impact future generations matters. The beautiful assurance is that the Lord restores things to a better position than they were before. He always provides an overflow when He restores. In the case of Nehemiah, what was originally in ruin was fully restored to a better position.

Question:

Where is restoration needed in your life? What do you think the Lord is asking you to do regarding that which is broken?

6

Hailstorms

Dare to live through adversity. Count it all joy when you suffer.

"Everyone then who hears these words of mine and does them will be like a wise man who built his house on the rock. And the rain fell, and the floods came, and the winds blew and beat on that house, but it did not fall, because it had been founded on the rock. And everyone who hears these words of mine and does not do them will be like a foolish man who built his house on the sand. And the rain fell, and the floods came, and the winds blew and beat against that house, and it fell, and great was the fall of it.' And when Jesus finished these sayings, the crowds were astonished at his teaching." (Matthew 7:24-28 ESV)

Adversity has a way of skewing our perspective and perception. It is hard to rejoice when it seems like life is falling to pieces. Yet, the bible tells us to count our sufferings, adversities, and trials as joy. (James 1:2-3) I always found this scripture interesting because there is a reason that the bible tells us to view adversity as a good thing. The outcome is that we become whole, we become complete, we lack nothing. That is what adversity does in the life of a believer. It further develops us and shapes our identity to align with who Jesus says that we are. The Lord has a way of helping us change our view of Him through adversity.

Human logic and instinct tells us to panic when adversity comes. Our flesh does not want to gain reason or perspective, it wants to react to survive. How do you rejoice when you have tears in your eyes? How do you rejoice when you're screaming and angry and frustrated and feel misunderstood within your soul because life continues to throw curveballs that you didn't see coming? The comforting news is that God uses everything that we go through to build us up; not one drop of suffering will be wasted. (Psalms 56:8)

"This hope we have as an anchor of the soul, both sure and steadfast, and which enters the Presence behind the veil, where the forerunner has entered for us, even Jesus, having become High Priest forever according to the order of Melchizedek."(Hebrews 6: 19-20)

Move actively, not passively during your storm. Watch for patterns and look for cycles. We cannot be idle and wait for things to mull over. We have to move in wisdom and operate in spiritual warfare regarding the things of God in our lives. We must go on the offense.

O-pen your mouth and speak the word of God over yourself. The enemy loves to silence your voice.

F-ilter your thoughts through the Holy Spirit. You are NOT defeated.

F-eel through your emotions. Process with the Lord and sound minded believers.

E-ncourage yourself though it is tough.

N-ote what the Lord says. Listen attentively.

S-urrender your will.

E-ncounter trouble with an attitude of praise, not pity. Rejoice from a place of victory even though you're in pain.

"For the weapons of our warfare *are* not carnal but mighty in God for pulling down strongholds." (2 Corinthians 10:4)

What is holding you back from fighting? Is apathy the barrier? Is fear? Identify what your storm consists of so you can fight. Declare war on your storm.

7

Aftermath

"To all who mourn in Israel, he will give a crown of beauty for ashes, a joyous blessing instead of mourning, festive praise instead of despair. In their righteousness, they will be like great oaks that the Lord has planted for his own glory." (Isaiah 61: 3 NLT)

When I first heard this scripture I would always wonder how beauty from ashes would look in my own life. After all, ashes derive from an object or item that has gone through some fire to the point where it no longer possesses recognizable features. Ashes do not provide a representation of status or affluence, but the simple truth of the fragility and vanity of humanity. When you examine ashes, there is nothing beautiful about them, or at least in my mind there was not. Ashes are piles of dust and to normal eyes, dust is nothing more than a mere mess waiting to be cleaned or removed. Yet, the bible promises that we will receive beauty for our ashes and joy for our mourning. We will receive the strength to praise and conquer heaviness. We will be stable as the people of God, but the key to the promise is going through the fire.

Fire has both positive and negative qualities. On the positive side, fire is used to sustain life. It is a resource that allows us to make food, it allows us to see in dark places, it serves as protection, and it is a transformative agent. Fire consumes what cannot stand in its presence. Fire devours what does not have the power to withstand its heat. God describes Himself as an all-consuming fire. (Hebrews 12:29) God is someone that completely changes your nature when you have an encounter with him. The encounters that we have with the Lord are meant to refine and purify us to produce holiness. Once that holiness is established, it completely changes the way you view and worship the Lord. (Psalms 96:9)

So how do we recognize the beauty that awaits? How do we remain hopeful until the promises of God manifest? Many times, we do not want to look at what has gone through the fire because sometimes it is just too painful. Examining the pain that we have gone through is key for finding the beautiful aspects of our struggles. Yes, that person broke your heart, but what can you glean from that experience? Sure, you did not get what you asked for, but what about all the priceless needs that were met in your life? There is always beauty in ashes and there is always something sweet that supersedes the bitter.

The Lord promises us that He will not put more on us than we can bear. (1 Corinthians 10:13) Often, we underestimate what we can bear by measuring it in our own strength and not in the strength of the Lord. We doubt how much of it God truly carries. We walk around *believing* that it is all on us. God wants to heal that mentality and silence the lies. He wants to heal that part of your soul that believes the burden is always on you so that you can walk boldly. Isaiah 61 is such a beautiful promise of the Lord for renewal after suffering. It reminds us of just how intentional and present the Lord is when we go through the pains of life. It also shows how the Lord uses us in the middle of our suffering to encourage and help others in their sufferings. It reminds us that there is a reward attached to our suffering. The Lord is aware and He totally, without a shadow of a doubt, cares. After the most unbearable circumstances, we are able to see the character of the Lord and why He chooses to develop His character in us. We are better able to digest the beauty that derives from our ashes of sorrow, pain, lack, uncertainty, and so much more.

Reflection:

Think about the times when you endured suffering. Try to identify how the Lord took the ashes of those situations and made them beautiful.

8

Flash Floods

"And I give unto them eternal life; and they shall never perish, neither shall any man pluck them out of my hand. My Father, which gave them me, is greater than all; and no man is able to pluck them out of my Father's hand. I and my Father are one." *(John 10:28-30 KJV)*

During heavy rainfall or thunderstorms, it is not uncommon to get a flash flood warning on our phones, computers, or televisions. What I have always found interesting about these warnings is that they are very detail-oriented and specific. These warnings delineate who the flash flood will affect, the anticipated damage, its occurrence (time/duration/expiration), and where it will occur. The warning is clear, but it is seldom that we experience the effects of a flash flood firsthand. Thus, the notifications and the warnings seem rather non-applicable to our lives because there is no tangible connection to the warning.

At times, life is just like a flash flood. Sometimes we are caught off guard by sudden moments of change. Sometimes we become numb to the warnings God gives us because we can only operate based upon our tangible, firsthand experiences. Sometimes we simply don't see the storm that is coming and we don't understand the severity. The good news is that Jesus is not caught off-guard by any of the sudden or flash flood moments in our lives. In fact, He has a habit of thriving in those moments. He has a trademark on performing miracles in the worst situations. We see waters surrounding us, threatening to take the very breath within our lungs and the Lord sees an opportunity for us to come to the end of ourselves. He sees an opportunity for us to walk in the miraculous with Him.

Genesis 7:7-20 is the story of the great flood. During this time on the earth, rain had never fallen. Noah was given a charge by God to build an ark and to take two of every animal both clean and unclean into the ark along with him and his family because a great flood was coming. For the people who had never seen rain, this mission that Noah was on was absolutely crazy. They probably thought he and his family were insane. Yet, Noah completed the mission that God gave him and was obedient. He heeded the warning that was given to him. When the rain came, he and his lineage were able to withstand it. The rest of the world that thought he was crazy, perished. It was only a flash flood warning to them, but not to Noah. There are a few things that can be taken away from this:

1. God always provides a way to endure.
2. God always prepares you for your flood, even in moments when they seem sudden.
3. God has a way of taking what is a flash flood to others and making it a new, life preserving opportunity for you.

Flash floods are only dangerous when we bypass the warnings and move in our own understanding. The temptation to fear will always be present in the midst of uncertainty. This does not mean that you cower--it only means that you reevaluate. God wants you to know that there is divine grace within your storm. This grace presents a unique opportunity for you to withstand and outlive the floods that will come. It is a promise that, like Noah, you will make it to a new place and a new season with a brand-new start in Him.

Affirmation:

When sudden moments happen to me, I will not cower in fear. I may feel fear, but it will not rule me. The Lord is my shepherd and I have everything I need. I will endure every flash flood that seeks to ruin my life. The Lord is faithful, and I will make it.

9

Clear Skies

"The disciples went and woke him up, shouting, 'Lord, save us! We're going to drown!' Jesus responded, 'Why are you afraid? You have so little faith!' Then he got up and rebuked the wind and waves, and suddenly there was a great calm." (Matthew 8:25-26 NLT)

Storms end.

Seasons change.

Life gets better.

Jesus calms the storm. Matthew 8 is a well-known passage of scripture and a prime example of the Lord calming a storm that was causing His followers to fear, doubt and panic. In this chapter, Jesus and His disciples are on a journey and they traveled by boat. On this night, they were caught in the middle of a tumultuous sea. There was so much turbulence that the disciples thought they were going to die. In a panic, they run to where Jesus is sleeping, and they wake Him up anxiously and fearfully. Jesus wakes up, reminds them that their faith needs to grow and commands peace to the storm. In an instant, the waves settle, the winds stop, and the storm ends. Similar to the storm that the disciples experienced in Matthew 8, so will your cares and worries settle. The anxiety and fear that you experience will dissipate and the purpose behind your storm will make sense. The winds will subside and waters will recede so that you will have peace.

Storms are scary, but they force you to reevaluate what's important in life. They cause you to reexamine where you expend energy and time. After finally making it through a season of hardship, you begin to appreciate the little things a lot more than before. The Lord does this on purpose. It is so easy for us to get caught up in the day-to-day hustle that we seldomly step back and truly appreciate the borrowed time that we live on. Storms have a way of providing revelation to the simple truth of life; that it is short and meant to be embraced.

Storms are used to agitate our lives so that we relinquish control of our wills and embrace the Lord's will. This is not always an easy process because our wills can look good, but only be good by the world's standards. If God is challenging you to release control to Him, then He must have something that is so much better and more fulfilling. As the skies begin to clear in your life, I challenge you to document your process. What is the Lord saying directly to you? What's being illuminated in your life towards your purpose and His will for your life? Write it down.[2]

---

[2] "For you shall go out with joy, And be led out with peace; The mountains and the hills shall break forth into singing before you, And all the trees of the field shall clap their hands. Isaiah 55:12 NKJV

10

A Graceful Storm

"What shall we then say to these things? If God be for us, who can be against us?"
(Romans 8:31 ESV)

Envision the end from the beginning. Picture yourself overcoming the challenges that want to drown you even if you must petition the Lord on the same issue and even if you have to face direct hostility. Elijah did this in 1 Kings 18. At this point in scripture, Elijah had been on the run. There were tons of people looking for him to no avail. Elijah willingly presented himself to King Ahab to prove that the God he served was the true and living God, not the idols that Ahab and Jezebel worshiped. Elijah held a contest to prove this. His actions resulted in the exposure and execution of the prophets of Baal, all 450 of them. This victory is important to note because between the oppressive rule of a wicked king and queen, famine and drought in the land, and rampant idolatry/hopelessness of many of the children of Israel, the odds did not look favorable. However, Elijah was bold and obedient. He faced his storm as the Lord led him which resulted in victory. The story then goes on to show how Elijah petitioned the Lord to end the drought in the land. Elijah went to the top of a mountain with his servant and prayed for rain, having his servant run back and forth to look at the sea for any signs of it. There were six no's before there was one yes. On the seventh time, his servant saw a little cloud, about the size of a man's hand. He saw something little that meant much. His servant rushed back and told Elijah and he instructed him to run ahead because he could hear the sound of an abundant rainstorm. He could hear the storm coming, but in this case, it was great news for them. Sometimes our storms look like a detriment but in reality, they are transitioning us from one season to another. The Lord sends little reminders along the way to remind us that we are moving forward.

We can find ourselves in this story at many points. The Lord may have us face our storms as we saw in the first portion of 1 Kings 18. He may have you face whatever seeks to take his spot in your life. He may challenge the hopelessness that you may feel during a storm. He may also have you challenge those that are in enmity towards you. The Lord may have you walk right into a storm, as he did in the second part of this scripture, so that the droughts and famines within your life end. Remember that your blessings may not immediately look like blessings. Enduring your storms gracefully means seeing yourself from the perspective of triumph. We're moving towards actualized victory. Every time you get up, Every time you pray, Every time you fast, every time you praise, every time you worship, every time you produce, every time you don't produce, every time you create, every time you obey, every time you repent, every time you pursue and the like: you are moving towards the goal that is Christ. The grace within the storm reminds you of the completed work of Jesus. When he hung his head on Calvary and professed it was finished, he meant it. We are merely catching up with time and the complete victory that belongs to us as children of God. (Philippians 3:13; 4:13)

Enduring your storm gracefully is not about being perfect in your emotions, affect, or demeanor. It is not about getting through the storm scrape-free. Enduring your storm gracefully is about trusting the Lord to lead and keep you while you battle YOU during trying times. It's not about getting it together, but it is about what God desires to develop in you for His glory. It's about exploring with the Lord and taking advantage of what your journey has to offer. It's not going to be pretty, but it is definitely worth it. The challenges that we face as the Lord cultivates us is not even comparable to the anointing that will come from being pressed. (Romans 8:18) As you go forward, you will become the graceful champion God intended for you to be from the foundation of the world. Embrace it. Live it. Be great.

Affirmation:

I am a champion within my storm. My storms are meant to develop me and not harm me. The Lord is present with me. I can do all things through Christ who gives me strength. I am a victor and I decree and declare that I will walk in my God-given identity as such. In Jesus' name, Amen.

[3] 1 Kings 18:41 NKJV

About The Author

Iniki is a thriving professional within the metro Atlanta area. After obtaining her Masters of Social Work (MSW) from Clark Atlanta University, Iniki has served in the realms of child advocacy, mentoring, and program development/support. She currently holds administrative roles and is the founder and creator of WildflowerKulture LLC., a project administration and planning business aimed to assist creative visionaries with organizing and structuring project goals to completion. Iniki hopes to help individuals cultivate their goals, bloom in unexpected places, and thrive in their full potential.

Made in the USA
Columbia, SC
13 May 2024